Gull Island Press

Advance the Engine Summer

by

Michael Leggs

Gull Island Press   **St. Paul, MN**

www.gullislandpress.com

Published by Gull Island Press
St. Paul, Minnesota

Manufactured in the United States of America

1st Edition

First Printing

Library of Congress Control Number: 2008902197

ISBN: 978-0-6151-9654-1

Acknowledgements

"When Wireless You Enter," "Decoder," "Monday Incorporated," and "The Death of Albert Flynstein" previously published in _The Argotist_ (Liverpool, England).

"This Umbilical of Light," "Liturgy," "Station-to-Station Madrid," and "Karmic Flight School Mid-Term Project" previously published in _Pith_ (Milwakee, WI).

"How to Install Hunger 2.0" previously published in _The American Drivel Review—A Unified Field Theory of Wit_ (Portland, OR).

"In Zeta Vitalis" is published in the fourth installment of the The No Record Press _Poetry Flyer_ (San Francisco, CA).

Special Thanks. . .

to all of those who have encouraged, inspired, and supported my creative
pursuits over the years.

Contents

Anima *11*

    Dandelion Conspiracy 12

    Semaphore 17

    This Umbilical of Light 18

    Hollow Houseguest at 2:38 a.m. 19

    Minnesota Nice 20

    Ghosts of Summer Frogs 22

    Misfit of Museo Vetrario 23

    Celluloid Orphan's Ode 24

    Yes, Chupacabra 25

    Reply 26

Imaginatio *29*

    Station-to-Station Madrid 30

    Bodies and the Stars 32

    Radioactive Showhorse Design 34

    When Wireless You Enter 36

    The History of Black 37

    I Was a Supercollider 39

    Frogs at the Alter of the Electric Orange 40

    The Death of Albert Flynstein 41

    Thursday Afternoon Was Broken 43

    Little Apple Lullaby 44

Conjunctio... *47*

   Liturgy.. 48

   To Ms. Matsuyama, As Dementia Comes Slowly 50

   Dodecaphonic High-Rise Disaster 52

   She Wears Cotton Balls Between Her Toes 53

   The Inverted Blue-Glass Bowl 54

   Desire.. 55

   Nighttime Travelers Across the Konza Prairie............................. 56

   Cathedrals of Spring... 58

   Dear, Princess Ephedrine... 59

   Jane Doe 60

Canaria.. *61*

   Winter on the Canine Internet 62

   Kismet 63

   On Days Like This When the Universe Blinks 64

   The Veterinarian's Lament 65

Circumiecti... *67*

   In Zeta Vitalis 68

   On This Blue Earth 70

   Snow Shovelling at Night.. 72

   Decoder 73

   Ode to the Coelacanth, 1938.. 75

   Good Morning, Columbus 77

   Freytag's Analysis of a January Day 78

   Un-Dream 81

Doctrinae *83*

Advance the Engine Summer 84

Monday Incorporated 85

How to Install Hunger 2.0... 86

How to Keep a Secret: Lesson 1... 88

Karmic Flight School Mid-Term Project.. 89

Anima

Dandelion Conspiracy

*Civilization is a conspiracy. Modern life is the silent
compact of comfortable folk to keep up pretences.*
                                                    —John Buchan

I. Decoding seas of living space

When I complain, it starts
to rain. *Hear the drops collide
and fall through the trees.*
I am convinced the lawn is just
an illusion pretending to be green
on the face of Earth. Beneath
lion's tooth blades, harvester ants hide
in a subterranean Mardi Gras town
of dismembered grasshopper hoedowns,
gypsy moth buffets, uncharted
in Brunfels' *Contrafayt Kreuterbuch*
where only herbals exist—
and roots are unillustrated.

II. The dog-faced boy muses and waits

The shot-gun circus is in town.
A clown conversation is muffled
by canvas, swaths of cigar smoke,
and the aroma of cotton candy. Across
the fairway in his trailer, Fedor IV,
the dog-faced boy, reclines

in a naugahyde chair imagining
young Master Spaulding's arrival —
a prerequisite to becoming immortal.

III. On a different plane the fortune-teller fails

Katarine conjures swirling convolutions
of a mariner's mind, crowned with jewels,
armed with a sphere of thread.

She specializes in relationship readings,
and asks: "Where did things go wrong?"
There is no vibration from the other
end of the line.
"Clairsentience and empathy escape me.
I must blanche these leaves as endive.
So long."

IV. The paper thin walls of the flop house vibrate with collective nightmares

This building is full of fools
who have keys to dimly lit rooms.
Tony Luna sleeps with his glock
in apartment 2A, face down
sitting at a kitchen table
strewn with Hustler® playing cards,
a dusting of coke, empty tomato juice cans

and one special bullet, a smiling
mini-Moai sculpted in its lead.

Across the hall, my sleeping room
is too oddly arrayed for sleep,
decked in icicles and droppers,
as dumb tra-la-la-las bound in the halls
in this school of underachievers.
The walls are expanding and contracting
—yes, breathing me to sleep in the belly
of Farmer Rackley's complex.

V. Field trip from Vattier across the divide

It was that piece of paper
—not a whole book— that helped me
see God, then cockroaches
in the tangerine light of the hallway
bathroom just before
the Swedish bikini team got dressed.

Five hours of climbing Mount Everest
under a conveyor-belt sky, and stepping
inside the uneven Claflin Mini-Mart
to buy Moon Pies. I am still alive.
Tomorrow I will sell plasma
and my Rolling Stones
"We Love You" 45 to pay rent.

VI. Despair is inevitable for one who has read
a little Sartre upon waking

I will disbelieve and forget all lessons
which are merely cap sears to be sent
in bouquets on an English Electric Type 1
to the farthest corner of the universe,
and tell myself that life begins
on the other side where, there,
I shall be the sum
of what I do not have.

VII. The resolution of a broken man is never pretty

I began this project to promote
and to protect the hypertext
of the unreal in a quest
for fleeting fame. Recognize
the suffocation is this
daily drill of negotiating
with ghosts, of wandering
alone at night, insomnia-rich
in continuous loops
mimicking Nobuko Miyamoto.
Reboot each morning
like an automaton.

VIII. Inevitably, nature has a way of deceiving even the sharpest mind

The blossoms in the yard imitate the sun.
I shall consume these for thirty days,
learn to lift the moss-covered stone,
and set off with black sails to Crete.

Semaphore

I float tethered by a thread

thin as a spider's web

to the funhouse floor

waiting for the proteins

to dissolve into dust and air,

fracture and give

way to the mad

birds' flight bending

gravity and luxury of time.

This Umbilical of Light

feeds me a facsimile of the Word
during this drowsy hour
of the early morning
from inside my T.V.
the evangelist evangelizes
and squints his eyes,
filling my shadowed living room
with a transmission of tears.
Although I don't feel susceptible
to his rantings about Jesus Christ,
I almost want to
swim to the telephone and call
the number on the screen
to see if he's really there,
(speaking tongues at 2 a.m.
somewhere between
Hollywood and Santa Cruz)
maybe start my day
by talking to a man in Pacific Time
who's got the Holy Ghost
and perfect hair.

Hollow Houseguest at 2:38 a.m.

I rattle through this hollow house

a worn apparition folding sheets of seem

in the detached atmosphere

of being and not

as time continues unawares,

expands and contracts

in odd intervals across

tracts of unconscious terrain

radiating in the minds of dreaming

cats and dogs persistently

dreaming until all

dreaming is done.

Minnesota Nice

I see Minnesota nice
in the middle of Frogtown
on Saturday night
      when I hail a Green & White
cab on University Avenue,
and dodge high hookers
riffling ghetto rolls

      when the Spaghetti Junction
crush of cars loosens on I-94,
finally lets me slide through
a sunshine traffic jam
—a celebrity walleye
swimming uptown
bound to sizzle
in some skillet
before I die

      when the Dorothy Day
contingent eats
after-bar omelets,
pancakes, and hash browns
in starvation dreams
hunkered in booths
at Mickey's Diner
with the slumming
Summit Avenue elite.

I see Minnesota nice

coursing the skyway's

hardened arteries

        pushing polar winds

while I spiral

  my way

 down

  to the city's

 core.

Ghosts of Summer Frogs

In the December evening
when atoms of light recede
into wisps of fog from the mouths
of howling dogs,
I know living,
and living cold.

I rake across the chain-link fence
against curtains of falling flakes,
slowly becoming less than snow,
a gross reduction of my plan.
Who would have known my life
would find me as the audience
to choirs, the ghosts of summer frogs?

I recall the story of the bluebird who sang
hymns to the farmer's wife's chagrin,
and how one May morning she removed
its tongue with a paring knife, dulled
from years of potato peeling.
Why did the song continue to live on
in muscle memory?

Such memory stirs this misery,
leaving unknowns hanging
as "x" and "y" ornaments
in trees too tense to turn green.

Misfit of Museo Vetrario

My life is blown like a fine piece of glass
cooling lopsided in the dim, foundry light.
I dreamt of being contoured, colorful, clean,
a millefiori vase, perhaps.
But that has never been.

I was rotated orange-hot around
rough cores of mud and dung
by some Altinum apprentice as practice,
(a means of learning lessons along the way)
who briefly went blank at the marver—
once, maybe twice—with the best intentions
while shaping my cooling skin.

Here I am, hardened and clear,
although envisioned a liter larger,
still able to imagine a shattering, a starting
over in the cradle of this Venetian lagoon,
centuries beyond Sutton Hoo.

I believe there is a plan
for imperfect bowls, off-kilter pitchers,
blistered mirrors, chipped chandeliers
asleep in soft cellars. That is why I keep
listening
      for footsteps
           on the stairs.

Celluloid Orphan's Ode

Frame by frame my images came
into existence and dissolved
in ancient reverberations
of reels across time,
brought into being
by duty or desire,
for reasons lost in haunted halls
in the minds of women and men,
some long dead.

Here I find the fortune
to be rescued and restored
as tranquil hands transform,
newly comprehend,
mend my fragile tapestries,
reframe and rename.

Here I rest,
wait for light to pass through
my shallow skin,
wait for the meaning
light will bring.

Here I sleep, dream,
live again
in occasional symposia
bridging beauty now
and beauty then.

Yes, Chupacabra

We know our goats lie
in your pastoral buffet
hollowed by daybreak.

Reply

When you ask me what I am
I should tell you
that I am
the result of Icarus' flight
toward the sun
if he had improved his wings
that I am
the darkness you find
as you descend
the stairs into your subterranean living
room
where the air is moist and hard
to breath
(but you should already know
that I will make you
uncomfortable)

When you ask me what I am
I should stare point blank
into my reflection cast
in the dimmest hemisphere
of your eyes
and project my ship of rage
onto the murky shores
of your curious continent
and proclaim: "I am the shining one
come to raze your soul!

Follow me to my world of fire!

You have no choice

in the matter!"

(but you should not be

surprised, for it

is you who have created this

lucent form)

When you ask me what I am

I should tell you that

I am

of two souls:

one that embraces the faint

whispering of dichotomous voices

in shades of white

and one that dreams of burning the canons of history

leaving the ashes of universal entropy

spinning around the bodies

of the living

who will lie pinned beneath the ruins

of the white-domed city

alive enough

to know that they are dying

When you ask me what I am

I will tell you that I am

of two rivers:

Yalu and Nile

that converge in my veins

and I will not be

ashamed to tell you

that I carry the passions

of two lands

in the current

of these incalculable moments

that expand in light of

your question.

Imaginatio

Station-to-Station Madrid

[Upon viewing Salvador Dalí's *Burning Giraffes and Telephones*]

It was the dime you put in the slot
that set the giraffes on fire.
Before you could dial the number,
your face changed and grew
smooth as the cover of a cigarette case.

A creature stands before you
on Baryshnikov legs
photographing the geography of your skin.
It's your skin he wants.
Your arms and hands become
spikes of tempered light.
"Reach for the receiver
and let your wispy veil slide down.
Leticia, let it fall. . .something
to remember you by as your youth
and beauty wane. . .Don't deny the wind
your leaves like an autumnless tree. . ."

You try to ignore his stare, and
apologize hoping that the Emersonian eye
with ganglia comprehends,
and try to reason
that all the things you feel are not real,
never happened to you,
never happen at all,

but you dare not cry,

for the tears

may bring on a comedy of black ants.

You hear the cosmodemonic whispers scraping:

"... *eres la objeta de mi cariño...*

siempre...no te lamentes cuando los ojos no existen..."

and try to speak until your mouth

surfaces again.

When your hands materialize,

insert another dime

and try to tune out the bleating

busy signals

of the burning giraffes.

Bodies and the Stars

I.

Vesta wades late September

in the stream just past midnight alone.

On the branch of a nearby birch

hangs her synthetic locks

subtracted from her head.

She caresses her smooth scalp

in the company of the constellations,

as countless palace fires

cast a sixty-watt glow

on her olive skin

and cool, current clouds

murmur white.

She pauses to divine the distance

between her body and the stars,

and hears a cadence

of broken leaves beyond the shore,

and reaches for a towel she stole

from the Dimeling Hotel

in Altoona last Fall.

II.

The sounds,

maybe the ominous settlings

of the constant dying fixtures

in a kitchen kingdom

full of luminous beings

lurking ankle high

on the linoleum unseen.

She stands motionless,

hip-deep in the stream

chanting the mantra she learned

to prevent the very yolk

from being sucked

from her head.

III.

Cyrus spies from behind the brush

transfixed and snickering

at the figure in the stream

(*that bulb full of fear*

 and insanity) unaware

of the candela of laughter

spinning silently like a Ferris wheel,

passengerless around his head.

Radioactive Showhorse Design

As its hooves hit the dust
its coat becomes a most brilliant green.
The scene, a delusional masterpiece,
dissolves around a Picasso pony come to life
on amphetamine haunches
beneath the jangling sun.

The weathercock begins to spin,
its metallic feathers licked
by the wailing benediction
of the serpentine wind that writhes
through windows and doors
of the the new-fallen ruins:
Joe Saint's, the hinterlands by the sea,
the burnt-sienna bronco sideways asleep
near shadows of rodeo flesh
corralled in a tangle.

The radioactive showhorse
breaks the imaginary fence,
and prances, gallops behind the parapet.
Spectators, feckless and still
smiling, swallow the show whole
and choke peacefully,
their countenances eaten
to renditions in bone.

A crowd of skeletons—
crotches turned to ashes,
pregnant with tranquility,
knuckles clicking—
remains
on melted, torn cushions
in the stands.
Their eye sockets whistle.
Their heads fill with rain.

When Wireless You Enter

It is not kind enough

to meet me

smile speechless

nightly

you promise to meet me

to walk to the corner

of my nightmare

and gently turn

down the thermostat

to seventy degrees

and let me continue to shed

my slow-motion skin

layer

by

layer

in the cool monotony

of the air-

conditioning

(backward to the dream:

Witness a widow sewing

a weakened pillow seam

headless)

muttering.

The History of Black

At first, there was nothing
and that nothingness grew
into the combination of all:
good, evil, and in between.

It started as a plant in a snowy field breaking
the earth and ice
climbing out of a crack in the blue earth, rising
in plumes of smoke.

Soon, green-thumbed hominids came along to tame
the fiery roots that rose
through winding, blue blankets of sky hung with honey
bees rapt in matrices of duty.

Spring sprang and summer came following after
dragging occasional rain
across latitudes of emptiness only known to the lonely
gardener of color wheels.

When the hummingbird hovered from color to color
sipping with seeming certainty
music streamed in binary code invisible as audible
aurea edulis consumed.

December came and swathed the hillside in white
rendering black as an idea,
a contradictory absence of substance, of soul
the gardener could not keep.

This was the history of black, the suggestion of a plant
misinterpreted in bodily form,
used in substitution of space when nothing is desired
for ham-fisted recipes.

Centuries later, Dr. Goebke stands on a soapbox
pandering to this absence
(as if addressing a monolith) promising medicine, money,
peace, architectured dreams.

This is the mystery of black, the resurrection of a theme
missing in physical form,
its hope invoked in soundbites, embraced by donkeys
from the machine.

I Was a Supercollider

Drifting beneath layers of sleep,
I dreamt my making into being
a collection of parts,
a major machine.

Of detailed design and early construction,
my circular accelerators sang
Faradian[1] fugues youthful
as a newborn babe
in the warmth of sub-atomic rain
at the end of the proton race.

[1] The story goes that, following a demonstration of the new miracle of electricity in 1831, Faraday was asked *"What use is it?"* He responded, *"Sir, of what use is a newborn babe?"*

Frogs at the Alter of the Electric Orange

Frogs at the alter of the electric orange

move caffeine molecules, the size of lily pads,

with telekinesis. It's one way to pass the time

before dreaming of flies.

The Death of Albert Flynstein

Today, I murdered a house fly.
I couldn't help it.
I just went bonkers
and was dead set on killing it
when it kept taunting me,
buzzing around my head.

So, I swung the flyswatter
and pulverized it
as it tried to take off
from the window sill.

I started thinking
about this fly's life,
and wondered if
he were important
in the fly world.

Maybe he was
the Albert Einstein
del mundo de musca domestica,
and after I killed him,
it sent shockwaves
through their news outlets.

He was probably on his way

to the fly post office

to mail his *Annus Mirabilis Papers*

to the *Annalen der Flysik*

when he met his demise.

Knowing house flies' rate of procreation,

it may be weeks before

they can speak or even dream

about the addition of velocities again.

Thursday Afternoon Was Broken

just like a coffee cup

(I found asleep

on the sidewalk)

that was dreaming

of a glue infusion

to hold it together

for that final drink.

Little Apple Lullaby

I could grow old here
cursing daily
the atmosphere that hangs about
this jaundice-light room
beneath the surface of earth,
counting cobwebs just after
they mysteriously materialize overnight
on the crumbling stucco ceiling,
as I deliberately degenerate
into drifts of broken hair
and flakes of skin
for countless seasons
tedious and on time.

I may entertain
the thought (not plan)
of immediately flying to Prague
to set up shop—maybe
a literary hamburger stand—
Yes! a burger and a book!
Or perhaps of playing
street-corner guitar for sporatic change
pitched into a battered case
but then again. . .

I could grow old here,

and become a small-town spectre

swathed in regret

woven from threads

of *What-if's* and *Shoulda-done's*,

while anticipating tuna salads,

melting Italian ice,

absence of Provalone,

and post-meridiem conversions of bread

into French toast.

I could grow old here reclining

in this uneven chair

watching charity happen

by the miracle of meter wave.

I could listen to the gravity-

vented furnace sigh and pang,

peal ruthlessly through

strata of sleep,

and imagine

how the Yeti secretly strides

backward against the Himalayan terrain,

afraid and unseen,

I could grow old here and dream.

Conjunctio

Liturgy

for my mother—Seoul, 1950

The drone of bombers
funnels through the night
in this hellish city
as we hang black curtains
over the windows of our house.
Whistles of light
arcing from the northern sky
remind me of life's worthless routine,
as mother and I crawl and hide
among the household furnishings
in this nightly ritual of assuming
the nature of shadows,
of pretending morning is a given,
and that this illness will pass.

Through a rent in the curtain I see
silhouettes hurry in all directions
worming from the windows
of the burning cable car
wearing wigs of fire,
wailing beyond decibels of belief,
pedestrian torches turning
in the blackness
the familiar fragrance
of acquaintances and friends
staggering toward the Temple of Heaven.

And through the veil of smoke

rising from the ruins

I see a man in bright array

rollicking on the rooftops,

in a fateful dance,

a revelry of havoc

deriding our existence.

To Ms. Matsuyama, As Dementia Comes Slowly

> "Memory is not an instrument for exploring the past
> but its theatre. It is the medium of past experience,
> the ground is the medium in which dead cities lie interred."
> —Walter Benjamin

I advise you to make your life's work

the work of remembering, at least

not forgetting the tiny shreds of living

you shall live. For there is no written rule

telling how to enter dementia's den.

Learn how to play

in a field of wits, and embrace

the art of forgetting how

to read faces, tones, timbres—

for now you are free

to make mystical choices.

Please rummage through

your funhouse kitchen searching

for hide-and-seek bowls

and disappearing spoons. Before

scolding the butter knife, wash

your hands

in the weeping sink.

If all else fails, I promise to wander

through subconscious locales to find you

dreaming on

a familiar city street of junction

and soul, near the lot

where your other home

burned down eleven times

a week ago.

Conversation will come easy

as we leaf through

photo albums remarking

on chubby-faced children

in stocking caps smiling,

the kind-hearted husband

who perished at Tay Ninh,

the daughter who becomes

your sister, then daughter

over and again.

We will talk telepathically

to spirits of dogs, who will

thank you in human voices

for treating them like toddlers.

We will enter your new house, and set

the dinner table in a delirious game of

plate, fork, space. . .

plate, fork, space . . .

Dodecaphonic High-Rise Disaster

—for A.B.

You were a song full
of notes that were no longer
able to cling
to the staves
but duty bound
to have an equal say.

Falling to the streets
below, they screamed
praying for a key
floating like lead
feathers, clawing
        and scratching
at balconies, rain-
soaked awnings,
vacant sun-
decks, cursing
the lack of musical bone.

Yes, you were
the song, and I became
a collector of brittle tones.

She Wears Cotton Balls Between Her Toes

like delicate fluffs of snow.

Each morning when we rise,

they lie scattered

about the bedroom floor

refusing to melt.

The Inverted Blue-Glass Bowl

sits on the turntable

and appears

to be a Portuguese hat.

I ask you

to put it on

and you do

for an instant

and comically

dance with the cat

by the oscillating fan.

The telephone rings.

The hat is

a bowl

again.

Desire

sashays in on red, crushed velvet paws

with blue and yellow striped claws

caked with time, space, and fragments of stars.

I recognize the click her lips make

when she cracks a smile,

and says, "It's time to go."

Nighttime Travelers Across the Konza Prairie

Pistons pound and hiss,

saying that this is

the wheel that was

once a stone, but now

technology has throttled time's neck

and I've carjacked eternity

            for a joyride

in a banana yellow '74 Buick Apollo

heading toward the edge of everything

past Nazarene churches

llama farms in the hinterlands

across prairieland composing

Konza songs farmers forgot how to sing.

Interstate 70 mutters like a jaded hooker

demanding the price of toll

centrifuging sex appeal

in a trailer park laboratory

softly speaking in Lucky Strike tones:

"When you grow old and tired of driving,

       sleep. . .

sleep in this bed.

      How much you got

for a date at the Dreamland Motel

in Junktown? Save some cash

for breakfast in Great Bend, or when

we party in Neodesha.

We'll have a slice of cold

apple pie in Blackwell, honey.

Just let go of the wheel

and coast — yes coast

into the Bible-Belt sea."

Cathedrals of Spring

On April nights
we weave nests of nonsense
          proclaiming this place
beneath richocheting
radio waves
a crossroad of intelligent life
          as we preen
in the northern lights'
green haze.

We are blind
city birds bathing
under street lamps
          engaging
in blue-nun banter
          pretending to perch
in electric pines

spinning songs
wearing minor-chord
feathers
mere spectres of lovers
dining on suggestions
spread across the night sky.

Dear, Princess Ephedrine

You were the reason
we split moments like atoms
in Mercury's dream.

Jane Doe

New York heroin

girl does Atlantic City.

Monkey: one. Girl: zip.

Canaria

Winter on the Canine Internet

Falling downward
the flakes find a place,
like the cryptic pieces of a jigsaw,
interlocking on Earth's frozen face,
to rest in banks by swing sets
and spiritless seesaws, melded
together under the cadence of paws
pounding the icy sidewalk.

Somewhere a lab-retriever logs on
browsing clickpaths comprised
of electrolytes left in sunny snow
and a discarded deer clavicle
that must be brought home.

Kismet

the star-

footed

black dog

walks

across

the snow

sniffing

making new

tracks

while

his snout collects

a beard

of white

flakes.

On Days Like This When the Universe Blinks

On days like this
when the universe blinks,
and garbage hounds creep
in the corners of dumps
to dine on chicken bones,
egg shells, and apple cores,
sleep is only logical. And like dogs,

lazy, sunrise sleepers nuzzle
through the gauzy flesh of dreams
hesitating before waking
afraid of confronting
gravity on canine streets.

The Veterinarian's Lament

My hands spread like rivers of brown leaves
across the belly of the dog that gives me
a knowing glance from eyes that speak
to mine with a sudden knowledge of true sleep,
while the catheter breathes a bright, green
snake of sodium phenobarbital
into arteries that, ten summers ago, coursed
with tennis-ball rhythms in licking grass,
knee high, waving
at rustic, swallowtail satellites.

This is how they usually go
—slowly in stages—
down the fuzzy staircase,
tip-toeing away from the hum
of flourescent laboratory lights toward
silly, swaying rainbow bridges
where rabbits dance among booda-bone
trellises decorated by chattering squirrels
in the beef gravy rain,
amid acres of ethereal farmland
conjured to challenge the reality
that dust is a destiny
as sure as bats
spiraling through
blankets of black.

Circumiecti

In Zeta Vitalis

Two dogs lie
like parentheses
on the couch
subordinating an extra idea
in some complex sentence
in this room of living
as particles
      of dust
          drift
             across
        degrees of dark
and slags
of light.

This is the space
that some dream of,
a space measured
in the glow of situation
comedies beamed in
high-definition satellite.

This is the space
—a space bound
by common fixtures:
dry pots of dumbcane,
lamps, ashtrays—

a space where

This is the American Earth

sleeps,

spine intact

in a jacket

sans illusions

of DNA.

On This Blue Earth

The snow is in cahoots with wind and ice,
composing songs for dances danced in silver cold
by maples, elms, brittle bee balm, clematis frozen,
involuntarily gamboling in white whirligig arrays
just before the sun reflects, declines, as if influenced by the weight of frost
spit out of wintry engines exhaling grey.

I will shovel, exfoliate the sidewalk making mounds, grey
piles of slush, audibly muttering "let's make a deal" to stubborn sheets of ice.
Maintenance of things, this house, the yard, the infinite frost
has helped me mark time, remember getting old, made life cold
in this annual subzero charade where winter pounds my life into sad arrays
of equations, systems of questions daring to be thawed, solved, re-frozen.

Each scrape of ice and snow and soot is frozen
and suspended in time as the day turns grey,
as waxwings sing songs and fly in arrays
against dishwater horizons and ice.
Deciphering these things is a job for cold,
blue-earth souls locked in offices of frost.

Today the Snow King sings songs cached in frost-
covered castles with signatures frozen
in three-four rime celebrating the cold
in carnivals and kettle corn turned grey.
There is no need for golden birds in ice.
There is no need for such feathered arrays.

Guilt washes over me for cursing this cold
Minnesota day, fixed in odd arrays:
ten thousand lakes, dead mosquitoes and grey
wolves traveling in packs in firs of frost
on Gully and Tenstrike tundra frozen,
hunting, howling across Tiger Lake ice.

In the cold, grey distance, arrays of frost-
faced lakes crack like secret puzzles frozen,
until spring solves all equations of ice.

Snow Shovelling at Night

St. Paul, Minnesota—February 11, 1997

The sidewalks have a need
to be uncovered
after each snowfall.
That is why I find myself
hovering over
this shovel
exfoliating ice
from the cement
time after time
imagining snowflakes
are angels
quietly descending
incandescent
to Earth
through the latticework
of air molecules
in the yellow silence
of this front porch light.

Decoder

When it's a short distance to the edge
of not knowing,
I find myself
standing, waiting here
in the corridors of night obscured
between layers of waking
and dreaming, waiting mute
and motionless, waiting
for the nothingness to find me
as I crouch, stone-faced
by the precipice, conjuring
like a mystic listening, envisioning. . .

A murder of crows arrives,
a formation of black,
magnetic heads on the horizon
arcing, zeroing in, deciphering
time through patterns of flight,
decoding dark and light,
folding inward,
detassling,
row by row,
golden-haired fields of flux. . .

Its shadow envelopes me

in a silence, a vacuum of non-thought,

inverse ideas, and ellipses trailing

off, traversing the black,

bridging the distance between

the clouds, revelling in the skies,

dissecting the palpable

silence with a sharper silence,

revealing the persistent

corollaries of loss hovering

in the cloud

of my palm.

Ode to the Coelacanth, 1938

See *Gombessa* swimming

          hollow spined,

singing aqua Zulu

     cave songs

         always blue—

playing

hide and seek

beneath

     the *Nerine,*

   Chalumna trawler

    navigating ages

unseen

bright and silent

as mountains

on the moon.

A one-hundred-quid

bounty spurs the poor

fishermen's pursuit

even though you are

unfit for a waltz

with wine.

While never lost,

you are found counting

backwards

fins across eyes

in cloaks of oil

treading time.

Good Morning, Columbus

The sun creeps upon the horizon,
a drunkened firefly out of its element,
as the wind combs the dogwood's green locks.
Through the venetian blinds, yellow rods of light
illuminate swirls of dust suspended
in the atmosphere of my underground study.

A dog's howl two doors down
fades into the rumble of a garbage truck engine
idling in the alley way.

It's Columbus Day, a day where no mail moves,
a day commemorating approximate discovery.

How Cristóbal Colón must have felt
arriving on the edges of known existence,
stepping on the shore of some tropical clime,
knowing or not knowing civilization,
not seeing the purple-throated carib poised
on atoms of salt and sea,
invisible, almost tangible,
somewhat psychic,
yet too quick to bleed.

Freytag's Analysis of a January Day

I.

This achromatic sky can only hold

so many things: two magpies, one shrike, a loon,

clouds woven as shrouds of grief,

the ache of bones forecasting low pressure. Soon

silverware and china will fall.

II.

During the snow emergency

last night, snowplows lurched

and grazed on cakes

of powder and crud.

Now we have this:

Across the street, an old woman

shovels her way out of drifts

piled past her creaking hips.

Yes, the world has been buried

alive, and all I will know for months

is white. How will I survive?

III.

Each morning, it is already

night. Each evening, dark

does a redundant dance.

The sun only comes

every now and then,

      and between

those visits, I resist

the urge to lean on SSRIs.

IV.

What is this package, dusted with

snow on the front porch steps?

A telescope from Edmund

Scientific? A new

set of c-h-a-t-t-e-r-i-n-g teeth?

A shipment of organics

from Puritan's Pride? My sanity,

wrapped in newsprint, drowning

in a pool of packing peanuts, perhaps?

V.

I have become the T.V.

The digital-living-room eye

and I

are one, and   I am

starting to shun sleep,

for there is

                    always

something (however

          insipid)

happening,

some. . .thing   hurtling

about the galaxy

                    toward

Earth,

                    somewhere

in the world,

somewhere

                    I am not.

Un-Dream

Shadow's sister Light

dances in a dream before

the absence of dreams arrives.

Doctrinae

Advance the Engine Summer

Advance the engine summer.
Dress cold window boxes in green
leaves to fill the rifts in
the unfolding of noon.

Record the incessant
rantings of brown birds
in bare trees religiously.
Forget winter verses bound
to melt soon.

Dare to measure swifts swooping in
systems of games
       —work and play.

Write a romance novel
to June
and have April proof
the galleys.

Lay crusts of stale bread
across the top
of the wooden fence
as days grow longer—and wait
for squirrels to wake
from sodden bunkers
in the alley.

Monday Incorporated

Wake to the slave-clock voice
from sound, chemical sleep.
Wipe the crust from your eyes.

Take the lightrail southbound
through nocturnal stations
toward your catacomb cube.

Ride shoulder to shoulder.
Engage in the frottage
and caffeine infusions.

Spew clichés from your mouth.
Exchange empty accounts
at lunch in Nightmare Café.

For the rest of the day,
fade into suggestions
of status quo cologne.

At five o'clock, head home.

How to Install Hunger 2.0

I.

Delete version 1.0 from hard drive.

Click "Set Up" and reboot brain to reconfigure

the neuronal response to phases

in metabolic status.

Be patient.

This may take several minutes.

Don't click twice.

II.

Defragment the lateral hypothalamus,

rename orbitofrontal cortex drive,

remap amygdalae, and deactivate

medial temporal lobes.

Working on other programs

is not recommended during

this process.

III.

Click "install," and "recommended setup."

Once program is installed,

click icon to start program.

Allow new operating system

to override craving for t-bone steak

with baked potato.

If craving persists, it may be necessary
to manually downgrade to Spam®
with liberal serving of government cheese.

IV.
If system is slow after downgrade,
go to administrative tools in "Control Panel"
and use satiety framework wizard
to rename "hunger" dynamic link library
to "low food security."
Reboot.

V.
If problems persist,
contact technical support
to speak to an appetite specialist,
who will walk you through
the reinstallation process,
or refer you
to a psychiatrist.

How to Keep a Secret: Lesson 1

Words perched in your ear

must not fly out of your mouth.

Clip their wings and smile.

Karmic Flight School Mid-Term Project

It's time to reverse
engineer despair like a
mathematical stunt.

Solve for two unknowns,
dissect the parabola,
always show your work

when plunging earthward,
mark the angle of descent,
flex post-vertex wings

as a butterfly
on the Pinneaple Express.
Find a place to land,

disassemble craft
and return to headquarters
to weave a new cocoon.

Study mutations
of flight on a lighted board.
Walk home in the dark.

www.ingramcontent.com/pod-product-compliance
Lightning Source LLC
LaVergne TN
LVHW011411080426
835511LV00005B/475